POETS

of
WORLD WAR I

RUPERT SMITH

Raintree is an imprint of Capstone Global Library Limited, a company incorporated in England and Wales having its registered office at 7 Pilgrim Street, London, EC4V 6LB – Registered company number: 6695582

To contact Raintree, please phone 0845 6044371, fax +44 (0)1865 312263, or email myorders@ raintreepublishers.co.uk

Edited by Andrew Farrow, Adrian Vigliano,
    and Diyan Leake
Designed by Philippa Jenkins
Original illustrations © Capstone Global
    Library Ltd 2014
Picture research by Mica Brancic
Production by Helen McCreath
Originated by Capstone Global Library Ltd
Printed and bound in China

ISBN 978 1 406 27328 1
17 16 15 14 13
10 9 8 7 6 5 4 3 2 1

Smith, Rupert (Poets of World War I)
A full catalogue record for this book is available from the British Library.

Acknowledgements
We would like to thank the following for permission to reproduce photographs: Alamy pp. 6 (Mirrorpix/© Trinity Mirror), 10 (© The Art Archive), 12 (© Maurice Savage), 18 (© The Art Archive), 20 (© The Art Archive), 31 (© Terry Harris), 34 (© The Art Archive), 36 (© Everett Collection Historical), 47 (© Mary Evans Picture Library); Corbis pp. 16 (© Bettmann), 28 (© Michael Nicholson); Getty Images pp. 8 (Hulton Archive/Phillips), 30 (Universal History Archive), 32 (Popperfoto), 39 (Picture Post/ Bill Brandt), 40 (Hulton Archive); Harvard University Archives p. 48 (HUD 3567.219.2, number 296); © Imperial War Museums pp. 22 (Every effort has been made to trace the copyright holder. The author welcomes any information regarding the copyright of this image.), 24, 26, 46 (The London Rifle Brigade Collection); OUCS p. 14 (Image provided by the Britten-Pears Foundation); Paul Barlow p. 50; Photoshot pp. 44 (© UPPA), 55 (© E.O. Hoppé); © The Royal Society p. 37; Shutterstock p. 4 (© Dziewul); SuperStock p. 53 (eps/Marka); Westminster Abbey pic p. 5 (Copyright Dean and Chapter of Westminster); The William Ready Division of Archives and Research Collections, McMaster University Library, p. 42. Vera Brittain material is included by permission of Mark Bostridge and T.J. Britain-Catlin, Literary Executors for the Vera Brittain Estate 1970.

Cover photographs reproduced with permission of Mary Evans Picture Library (Süddeutsche Zeitung Photo) and Shutterstock (© Elena Elisseeva).

CONTENTS

Any words appearing in the text in bold, **like this**, are explained in the glossary.

"My subject is war"

World War I was one of the bloodiest conflicts in modern history – and yet it produced some of the best poetry of the 20th century. Many people's first encounter with poetry is through writers like Wilfred Owen and Siegfried Sassoon. The passion and power readers find there makes a very deep impact on them.

THE SHOCK OF WAR

What was it about the war that created such a lot of important poetry that we keep coming back to a hundred years later? There are three main answers to that question. First, World War I crashed into a world absolutely unprepared for slaughter on that scale. It was the first total "modern" war. It was fought with tanks and machine guns that were capable of wiping out tens of thousands of men in a day. At the time, much of the poetry was supportive of the war. But most of the war poetry we read today recorded the shock and disgust people felt for the sort of violence that sadly we now take for granted.

Second, the young men and women who wrote about the war were a very talented group of people. They were the product of a rich period of English literature who suddenly found themselves inspired by an incredibly urgent subject matter. They wrote about it with great passion, from first-hand experience, but also with great artistry. They created work that spoke not only to readers at the time but also to later generations.

PAIN INTO POETRY

Third, and perhaps most importantly, the war poets focused on issues that continue to matter to us today. They talked about the human cost of war and how politics played its part. They challenged the government, the public, and even the armed forces to justify the death and suffering of many millions.

When we read a poem like Owen's "Dulce et Decorum est", Sassoon's "Counter-Attack", or Rosenberg's "Break of Day in the Trenches", we wonder how governments can possibly justify the wars that continue to plague our world. Some war poets – such as Owen, Rosenberg, Brooke, and Sorley – died young. Some lived on, like Graves, Sassoon, and Brittain. But they all summed up in their poetry the terror of fighting and witnessing destruction on a massive scale. Their voices will continue to be heard as long as nations find themselves at war.

Memorial stone in Westminster Abbey, London, commemorating World War I poets. Owen's famous quote (see below) is in red.

LINK
See a large collection of material at The First World War Poetry Digital Archive: www.oucs.ox.ac.uk/ww1lit

"My subject is War, and the pity of War. The Poetry is in the pity ... All a poet can do today is warn. That is why the true Poets must be truthful."

Wilfred Owen, **"Preface"** (1918)

MAJOR THEMES

What was it like to live through World War I? Poetry is one of the most important records of how people felt about the life-changing events. As we read the poems, we see that there are some subjects that come up again and again. These were often things that were new, and shocking, to soldiers fighting at the front and to the people back home.

Sacrifice and glory

In the early months of the war, many men felt that joining the fight gave them a chance to do something wonderful for their country. Death was a small price to pay.

Soldiers in a trench near the Somme River prepare for a gas attack with protective masks.

> " I am in a unit in the Great War, doing and suffering, admiring great endeavour and condemning great dishonour. I may be dead before this reaches you, but I will have done my part. Death is as interesting to me as life. "
>
> Francis Ledwidge, Irish poet (1887–1917), written six months before his death at Ypres, Belgium[1]

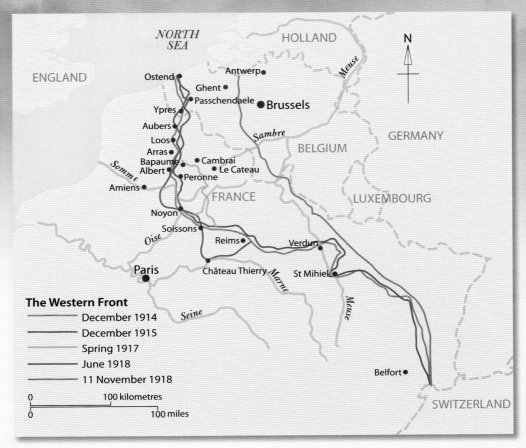

The Western Front

——— December 1914
——— December 1915
——— Spring 1917
——— June 1918
——— 11 November 1918

0 — 100 kilometres
0 — 100 miles

Trench warfare, shell shock, grief

World War I became a different type of fighting to anything seen before. The opposing armies dug into muddy trenches for many months, and used barbed wire, **poison gas**, and machine guns. New inventions, including aircraft and tanks, gave them more efficient ways of killing each other.

Nearly all of the poets in this book served on the Western Front – a line of trenches stretching from the North Sea coast of Belgium down through north-eastern France to the Swiss border. Many of the main battles of World War I were fought along this line in an attempt to halt German advances into France.

The **psychological** effects of trench warfare were unexpected and frightening. Many thousands of men were hospitalized with **shell shock**.

A few people, like the poet Charles Sorley, anticipated the horror of war. Most were unprepared for the scale of death and the grief that came in its wake. As a whole generation went to the slaughter, the mood of optimism turned to despair.

7

TIMES OF CHANGE

The years leading up to World War I saw incredible, rapid change. The **British Empire** was at its height, with money pouring in from all over the world. In other industrial nations, such as the United States and Germany, people were enjoying increased prosperity. But political unrest was threatening the foundations of societies all over the world. This eventually led to the great shock of the **Russian Revolution** in 1917. The old way of life, where the upper class had all the money while the working class did all the labour, was breaking down. Better health and education encouraged ordinary people to demand better living standards for themselves and a greater share of the wealth. Women in Europe and the United States were campaigning for the right to vote. Many writers looked forward to war as a way of shaking up society even more and making a fresh start.

Nothing, however, could prepare people for the reality of what became known as the Great War.

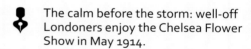

The calm before the storm: well-off Londoners enjoy the Chelsea Flower Show in May 1914.

THEN and NOW

Life was very different in 1914. Life expectancy was a lot lower and there were hardly any cars on the road. Women couldn't vote and many of the freedoms that we take for granted today were a long way off. Here are some of the key facts about life in the United Kingdom then and now.

	Population	Life expectancy (years)	Women in work (%)	Average annual household income
1914	42,000,000[2]	53[4]	24[6]	£51[8]
Now	63,000,000[3]	79[5]	65[7]	£30,000[9]

A new type of war

There had been recent, bloody conflicts with enormous loss of life. The American Civil War (1861–1865) was still fresh in the memory for the older generation, and the Boer Wars ended as recently as 1902. But those wars were nothing compared with World War I. The scale of death was unimaginable – and this was partly due to new technology. Machines were providing employment for millions, better transport, and an easier way of life. But they were also creating new, more efficient ways of killing others. Tanks, machine guns, poison gas, and aerial bombs replaced rifles and swords as the tools of modern war.

It was also hard to work out what the fighting was for. A few yards of mud in north-east France? What did that matter to anyone? Things were very different in World War II, when people understood the threat of Hitler. But to a soldier in 1916, facing certain death in the trenches, progress seemed slow and the results uncertain. Religion was breaking down, church attendance was plummeting, and the war seemed to confirm that we were living in a godless world. After the horrors of the **Western Front**, nothing would ever be the same again.

> **LINK**
> Find out more about pre-war life at www.nationalarchives.gov.uk/records/census-records.htm

WILFRED OWEN

Born: Oswestry, Shropshire, 1893
Died: Ors, France, 1918

Wilfred Owen wrote some of the most famous poems of World War I, including "Anthem for Doomed Youth", "Dulce et Decorum est", and "Strange Meeting".

DID YOU KNOW?
Owen was killed just one week before the end of the war.

Wilfred Owen was 25 when he died in France.[10] He spent a total of four months in active service, of which not more than five weeks were at the front line. But despite his youth and relative lack of experience, Owen has become the best known of all the war poets – and his reputation keeps on growing. More than any of his **contemporaries**, he represents the tragedy, the anger, and the terrible sense of waste that draws us back to the war poets a hundred years later.

BEFORE THE WAR

Wilfred was the oldest of four children. His father was a railway employee who struggled to provide for the family. When he was 14, the family moved to Shrewsbury. The teenage Wilfred developed an interest in poetry, especially the work of Keats and Shelley.

Wilfred's parents couldn't afford to send him to university and so he took up an unpaid job as assistant to a vicar in Dunsden, near Reading. Under the influence of his very religious mother, he was thinking of becoming a church minister.

WRITING ON THE FRONT LINE

Owen eventually left the vicarage to work as an English teacher in France. The outbreak of war found him in Bordeaux, cultivating friendships with French poets and writing his own work in his spare time. In September 1915, a full year after the start of the war, Owen could stand aside no longer. He returned to England and **enlisted**. "I don't imagine that the German War will be affected by my joining in," he wrote to his cousin Leslie Gunston, "but I know my own future Peace will be." [11]

For the next 14 months, he trained as an officer. It wasn't until the end of 1916 that he was finally posted to France on active service. He was **commissioned** as a second lieutenant with the Manchester Regiment, a junior officer leading his men in the very worst of the fighting.[12] For two short, intense periods – winter 1916 to spring 1917, and summer to autumn 1918 – Owen witnessed the horrors of trench warfare (see page 14). He was still writing all the time, sending poems home in letters to his friends and family in England.

Getting recognized

Owen was regarded by his admirers as a writer of great promise. But it was only after the end of the war that his friend and champion Siegfried Sassoon edited and published the first collected edition of Owen's work. His poetry has never been out of print since then.

> "One of Christ's essential commands was: Passivity at any price! Suffer dishonour and disgrace; but never resort to arms ... Be killed; but do not kill ... And am I not myself a **conscientious objector** with a very seared conscience?"
>
> Letter from Wilfred Owen to his mother, Susan Owen (May 1917) [13]

LINK
The Wilfred Owen Association has information and news about Wilfred Owen's life at **www.wilfredowen.org.uk**

OWEN'S WAR

Owen's first experience of action was on the River Somme, France, in January 1917. The **Allies** were holding a stretch of **no man's land** in Beaumont-Hamel. It was a dangerous place for an inexperienced young officer to be. "I have suffered seventh hell," Owen wrote to his mother. "I have not been at the Front. I have been in front of it."[14]

Away from the protection of the trenches, he led his men across a hell of mud – "not sloppy mud, but an octopus of sucking clay, 3, 4, and 5 feet deep, relieved only by craters full of water. Men have been known to drown in them." They took refuge in a dug-out (a hole in the ground used as a temporary shelter) while the Germans shelled them. "My dug-out held 25 men tightly packed. Water filled it to a depth of 1 or 2 feet, leaving say 4 feet of air." Owen survived, but witnessed terrible **carnage**.

Ill health and injury

Over the coming months, Owen suffered from concussion and ill health from the cold, wet conditions as he was sent repeatedly to the line. Finally, on 12 April 1917, he was hit by a shell. He spent several days sheltering in a hole with the remains of a dead officer.

Owen was diagnosed with **shell shock**. He was evacuated to the Craiglockhart War Hospital near Edinburgh to recover. It was during this time that he met Siegfried Sassoon (see page 15).

Owen's grave in the communal cemetery in Ors, northern France, close to the spot where he was killed.

12

LINK
To find out more about what life was like in the trenches, see www.nationalarchives.gov.uk/education/greatwar/g3

"The sensations of going **over the top** are about as exhilarating as those dreams of falling over a precipice, when you see the rocks at the bottom surging up to you. I woke up without being squashed. Some didn't."

Letter from Wilfred Owen
to his brother Colin (14 May 1917)

Owen was discharged from hospital in October 1917 and he considered looking for a home posting for the rest of the war. However, Sassoon's decision to return to the front convinced Owen to rejoin his regiment in France. Sassoon was wounded, and Owen was determined to carry on his work: "Now must I throw my little candle on his torch, and go out again."[15] He left England on 31 August 1918, never to return.

Brave ending

The fortunes of war were changing. Germany's final offensive had failed and the Allied forces were pushing them towards surrender. Owen was in the thick of it and was awarded the **Military Cross** for his bravery in battle. He continued writing, sending his final batch of poems to Sassoon in September. It included **"Spring Offensive"**, one of his finest poems.

Owen was killed during an assault on the Oise–Sambre canal near Ors, France, on 4 November 1918. A telegram bearing the news of his death reached his family a week later, on **Armistice** Day.

DISCUSSION TOPIC

Why did Owen fight?
It is obvious from his poetry that Owen was disgusted by the war. Yet he not only enlisted in the first place but returned to the battlefield after recovering from shell shock. Why do you think he went back to France?

OWEN'S POETRY

One of the reasons why Owen remains the most popular of all the war poets is his talent for putting complex, painful ideas into simple but powerful language. His religious background equipped him with imagery that he used to great effect and war gave him his subject matter.

The poems from Owen's early trench experience, such as "Greater Love", are highly **romantic** and emotional. The turning point in his style came when he met Siegfried Sassoon in August 1917. Sassoon encouraged Owen to write in a harsher, more direct style, and to abandon the lush imagery of earlier work. The effect was immediate.

An original manuscript written by Owen in 1917, showing Sassoon's notes and suggestions. The word *Dead* in the title was later changed to *Doomed*.

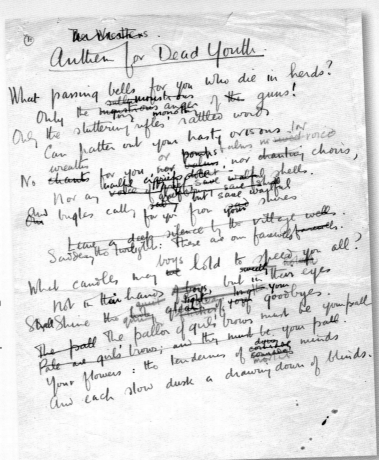

LINK

Find out more about how Owen wrote his poetry at the British Library website: www.bl.uk/learning/langlit/changlang/writtenword/owenpoem/owenhome.html

> "Gas! GAS! Quick, boys! – An ecstasy of fumbling,
> Fitting the clumsy helmets just in time;
> But someone still was yelling out and stumbling,
> And flound'ring like a man in fire or lime...
> Dim, through the misty panes and thick green light,
> As under a green sea, I saw him drowning."

"Dulce et Decorum est" (1917)

Rage and grief

The poems that Owen wrote in the last 15 months of his life were brutal, sometimes funny, often heartbreaking. He used the real speech of soldiers: "I'll do 'em in," says the soldier in "The Dead-Beat", the first poem he wrote "in Sassoon's style".[16] His first masterpiece, "Anthem for Doomed Youth", was written in Edinburgh in September 1917. In 14 lines, it expresses the rage and grief that Owen felt after witnessing the slaughter of his comrades.

Owen came to hate the false **patriotism** that was sending young men to certain death. He expresses this idea in his angriest poem, "Dulce et Decorum est". It portrays the horrific events of a gas attack before challenging the reader to repeat "the old lie" in the title – "*Dulce et decorum est pro patria mori*" (or "How sweet and right it is to die for one's country"). This and Owen's final poems, including "The **Show**", "S.I.W.", "Mental Cases", "Strange Meeting", and "Spring Offensive", are among the most famous works not just of the war, but of 20th-century English poetry.

OWEN AND SASSOON

Owen meeting Siegfried Sassoon in 1917 is one of the key moments in the history of war poetry. Owen knew of and admired Sassoon's work – "I am not worthy to light his pipe", he wrote to his mother.[17] But later, Sassoon admitted that perhaps Owen was the greater poet.[18] Their friendship has inspired many writers, including Pat Barker, whose 1991 novel *Regeneration* was made into a film starring James Wilby as Sassoon and Stuart Bunce as Owen.

SIEGFRIED SASSOON

Born: Matfield, Kent, 1886
Died: Heytesbury Hall, Wiltshire, 1967

Siegfried Sassoon was a fierce critic of the war who expressed his anger, sorrow, and frustration in some of the most powerful poetry of the period.

DID YOU KNOW?
Sassoon survived the trenches and wrote several best-selling books after the war. He lived to the age of 80.

Siegfried Sassoon came from a rich, upper-class family in Kent.[19] His early life was idyllic – he didn't start school until he was 14, and he seemed more interested in playing cricket, hunting, and writing poetry than getting any qualifications. The only clouds on the horizon were the break-up of his parents' marriage and the death of his father. However, he inherited a lot of money from his aunt and lived the life of a wealthy country gentleman.

The outbreak of war in 1914 jolted Sassoon out of his comfortable existence. He **enlisted** straight away. The conflict touched his family deeply as his brother Hamo was killed at **Gallipoli** in 1915. Sassoon quickly established a reputation for bravery (his men nicknamed him "Mad Jack"). He recorded his impressions of war in his poems.

"FINISHED WITH THE WAR"

Sassoon's attitude to the war changed quickly. At first he was as enthusiastic as everyone else, but by 1916 he had become critical of the fact that soldiers were being sent to certain death. During a stay in England in 1917, Sassoon wrote a letter to his commanding officer under the heading: "Finished with the War: A Soldier's Declaration". "I am making this statement as an act of wilful defiance of military authority, because I believe that the war is being deliberately prolonged by those who have the power to end it," he said.[20] The letter was printed in newspapers and read out in Parliament. Sassoon narrowly avoided being **court-martialled**. He was sent instead to Craiglockhart War Hospital in Edinburgh, officially suffering from **shell shock**.

The scandal made Sassoon famous. His war poems, mainly published in 1917 and 1918, sold widely. In 1919, Sassoon left the army. Later that year, *War Poems* was published, sealing his reputation as the most critical and **satirical** of all the poets of the period.

After the war, Sassoon suffered from depression. It was not until 1928, with the publication of the autobiographical *Memoirs of a Fox-Hunting Man*, that he once again found his feet as a writer. Despite the success of his books, he was unsettled and unfulfilled, and had a string of failed relationships. In 1951, he received the award of Commander of the Order of the **British Empire** (the third highest honour for service during World War I). Sassoon died in 1967 at the age of 80.

LINK
Read more at the Siegfried Sassoon Fellowship: www.sassoonfellowship.org

"I believe that this war, on which I entered as a war of defence and liberation, has now become a war of aggression and conquest."

"Finished with the War:
A Soldier's Declaration" (1917)

HERO OR TRAITOR?

Sassoon was 27 when war was declared,[21] and with his upper-class background it was obvious that he would be **commissioned** as an officer. In 1914, he enlisted as a trooper in the Sussex Yeomanry, but by 1915, he was a second lieutenant with the Royal Welch Fusiliers. He was sent almost straight away to France where he immediately became a hero to his men for rescuing a wounded lance-corporal under heavy fire. For this action, Sassoon was awarded the **Military Cross.** Later that year, he took a German trench single-handedly, and was recommended for the highest military award for bravery, the Victoria Cross.

> "As I stepped over one of the Germans an impulse made me lift him up from the miserable ditch... He didn't look to be more than 18. Hoisting him a little higher, I thought what a gentle face he had, and remembered that this was the first time I'd ever touched one of our enemies with my hands."

Description of the Battle of the Somme, *Memoirs of an Infantry Officer* (1930)[22]

Sassoon's attitude to the war changed in 1916, when he witnessed the first **Battle of the Somme** in July and the bloody Battle of Arras in April of the following year. These experiences, combined with the deaths of people close to him, made Sassoon question the war. While recovering from his injuries in 1917, Sassoon decided that his duty as a writer was to tell people in Britain about the pointless **carnage** he'd witnessed.

Changing his mind

Many people branded Sassoon a traitor for opposing the war, but nobody could question his bravery. Sassoon himself rejected the title of hero – he threw the ribbon from his Military Cross medal into the River Mersey, Liverpool, intending never to return to battle.[23] But he changed his mind while he was in hospital, and in November 1917, he was declared fit for "General Service" and returned to duty. He stayed at the front line in France until July, when he was shot in the head by a British soldier who had mistaken him for a German.[24] The wound was not serious, but bad enough to end his active service.

DISCUSSION TOPIC

Was Sassoon a traitor?
Sassoon published outspoken criticism of the war, and the people who were running it in the government and the army, at the height of conflict. Was he right or wrong to do so? Would it have been different if someone had made the same criticisms in World War II?

LINK
Find out more about Sassoon's wartime experiences at the War Poets Association website: **www.warpoets.org/conflicts/greatwar/sassoon**

THE RELUCTANT WAR POET

The label "war poet" annoyed Siegfried Sassoon, who wrote poems both before and after World War I. However, he is best known for his hundred or so poems that deal with the war. Wilfred Owen regarded him as a hero and an inspiration, "the Greatest friend I have".[25] Sassoon's angry, satirical verse defines what we now think of as war poetry.

Sassoon started writing poetry in his teenage years, and attracted the attention of influential critics and editors – but he realized that he had not yet found his true subject matter. That came with the war, and the shocking death of his brother Hamo and close friend David Thomas, both of whom he commemorated in poems ("To My Brother", "A Subaltern", "The Last Meeting").

Sassoon met the poet Robert Graves while on duty in France in 1916. Graves encouraged Sassoon to write in a more direct, less "poetic" style, just as Sassoon did with Owen a year later. Sassoon began reporting what he saw in a vivid, factual way – the best way, he thought, to bring his message to readers back home. He wrote "Died of Wounds" in hospital at Amiens in 1916. It is a brief, brutal description of a delirious young soldier's final hours.[26] "They" (1916) was written in a late-night fit of anger: "George lost both his legs; and Bill's stone blind; / Poor Jim's shot through the lungs and like to die." Even Sassoon's editor, Edward Marsh, thought it "too horrible".[27]

British soldiers going over the top in the Battle of the Somme, as described in Sassoon's poem "Attack".

PACIFISM IN WORLD WAR I

Not everyone believed that war was justified, and some people refused to fight. This meant they were breaking the law – and many of them ended up in prison as a result. Many thought they were cowards, but there was a growing number of prominent figures in Europe and the United States who believed in **pacifism** – peace above all else. Today, some people choose to wear white poppies instead of the traditional red, as a way of remembering the dead while expressing their opposition to war.

"COUNTER-ATTACK"

Sassoon published many of his most important pieces in two books, *The Old Huntsman* (1917) and *Counter-Attack* (1918). Even before the scandal of "Finished with the War" (see page 17), these poems were a shock to readers. "Attack" (1917) remains the most powerful expression of going **over the top**. "Counter-Attack" (1917) perfectly summed up Sassoon's anger at the waste of life. After a horrific, dramatic account of trench warfare ("The place was rotten with dead"), he watches another soldier bleed to death before recording, in the last line, "The counter-attack had failed."

One of Sassoon's last war poems, written after the **armistice**, is "Everyone Sang" – proof that he could write about more than just misery. It ends very sadly: "the song was wordless". Yet his joy at the end of the war ("I was filled with such delight / As prisoned birds must find in freedom") is a rare moment of light in the very dark landscape of his work.

> "Lines of grey, muttering faces, masked with fear,
> They leave their trenches, going over the top,
> While time ticks blank and busy on their wrists,
> And hope, with furtive eyes and grappling fists,
> Flounders in mud. O Jesus, make it stop!"

"Attack" (1917)

LINK
Listen to recordings of Sassoon reading his war poetry at The Poetry Archive:
www.poetryarchive.org/poetryarchive/singlePoet.do?poetId=1561

ISAAC ROSENBERG

Born: Bristol, 1890
Died: Fampoux, France, 1918

Isaac Rosenberg overcame ill health and a lack of education to become one of the most important poets of the war before his death on the Western Front.

DID YOU KNOW?
Rosenberg enlisted in the **Bantam** Battalion of the 12th Suffolk Regiment because it was for men under 1.6 metres (5 feet, 3 inches) tall.

Isaac Rosenberg is the odd man out among the war poets. The son of **Jewish immigrants**, he grew up in poverty in the East End of London. He was a small, sickly **pacifist** who only **enlisted** because his soldier's pay would keep his family from starving.[28] He was also a talented artist. His poems are often described as difficult and obscure – and yet Rosenberg is now considered among the best of the war poets.

EARLY LIFE

Isaac was the son of a pedlar who fled Russia to raise his growing family in England. In 1897, the family moved to Cable Street in Stepney, London, where both parents and five children slept in one room.

Isaac had a gift for painting and drawing, but he had to leave school at 14 to start earning money. He became an apprentice engraver and went to evening art classes. In 1911, he gained a place at the famous Slade School of Fine Art.

POET OR PAINTER?

Throughout his time at the Slade, Rosenberg was writing as well as painting, but he was never confident about his literary talent. "I really would like to take up painting seriously," he wrote in 1910, "I think I might do something at that; but poetry – I despair of ever writing excellent poetry."[29] By the time Rosenberg left art school in 1913, he'd attracted the attention of Edward Marsh, the powerful editor of the book *Georgian Poetry*, which included work by Siegfried Sassoon and Rupert Brooke.

In 1914, Rosenberg travelled to South Africa to recover from the chronic bronchitis that affected him all his life. The warm weather helped, but he was unlucky – war was declared, and he returned to England. He enlisted and was posted straight to the Somme in 1916.

Rosenberg was 27 years old when he died. His poetry was just starting to gain international recognition. Rosenberg himself believed at the end of his life that he was "more deep and true as a poet than painter".[30] His most enduring work was not published until years later. His paintings now hang in some of the most important galleries in the world.

"I think that poetry should be definite thought and clear expression, however subtle; I don't think there should be any vagueness at all; but a sense of something hidden and felt to be there."

Letter from Isaac Rosenberg to Edward Marsh (1917)[31]

LINK
Find out more about Rosenberg's art, and other artists in his circle, at the National Portrait Gallery website: **www.npg.org.uk**. Type "Rosenberg" into the search box.

AN UNKNOWN GENIUS

Some of Rosenberg's poems and **fragments** were published before his death, but it wasn't until 1937, with the publication of his *Collected Works*, that he became widely read. Siegfried Sassoon was a great admirer of Rosenberg's poetry. He wrote a foreword to the book, hoping "to gain for him the full recognition of his genius which has hitherto been delayed." [32]

The Road, a 1911 painting by Rosenberg from around the time he started training at the Slade art school.

Rosenberg realized that his work wasn't to everyone's taste. He wrote in a letter in 1915: "Most people find my poems difficult. My technique in poetry is very clumsy, I know."[33] Rosenberg was deeply immersed in Jewish culture and history and at first he focused on Biblical themes.

The war gave Rosenberg a much more urgent subject matter. It also forced him to use a more direct style: writing at the front, he just didn't have time to polish his poems. "You can only, when the ideas come hot, seize them with the skin in tatters raw, crude, in some parts beautiful, in others monstrous."[34]

WRITING IN THE TRENCHES

Between 1915 and his death in 1918, Rosenberg wrote the poems that made him famous after he died. Sassoon, among others, considered "Break of Day in the Trenches" to be one of the best poems of the war. It's a strangely calm, intimate piece of writing that sums up Rosenberg's approach. He focuses on a rat that runs across his hand: "You will do the same to a German / Soon, no doubt." As he watches the rat disappear across **no man's land**, he wonders, "What do you see in our eyes / At the shrieking iron and flame". Finally, Rosenberg picks a poppy from the top of the trench and sticks it behind his ear – a simple act of defiance to the horror that would soon claim his life.

His poems "Louse Hunting" and "Dead Man's Dump" equal in power anything by Owen or Sassoon. They suggest that Rosenberg was capable of achieving great things. Sassoon wrote, "I see the poems he might have written after the war, and the life he might have lived when life began again".[35] Sadly, unlike Sassoon, Rosenberg never had the chance to prove his potential.

> "The air is loud with death,
> The dark air spurts with fire
> The explosions ceaseless are.
> Timelessly now, some minutes past,
> These dead strode time with vigorous life,
> Till the shrapnel called 'an end!'"
>
> "Dead Man's Dump" (1917)

DISCUSSION TOPIC

Rosenberg the outsider

Unlike most of the British war poets, who were middle-class Englishmen, Rosenberg was a working-class Jew, a private rather than an officer. How did his "outsider" status influence his poetry? Can we tell from reading his work that he was from a different background?

"I have joined this Bantam Battalion (as I was too short for any other) which seems to be the most rascally affair in the world. I have to eat out of a basin with some horribly smelling scavenger ... Besides my being a Jew makes it bad amongst these wretches. I am looking forward to having a bad time altogether."

Letter from Isaac Rosenberg to his friend Sydney Schiff (October 1915)[36]

Casualties in the Battle of the Somme[37]	
Nationality	Numbers
British	Approximately 420,000
French	Approximately 195,000
German	Approximately 650,000

Battle fatigue: men of the Warwickshire Regiment rest during the Battle of the Somme, their rifles stacked nearby. Exhaustion and **shell shock** put many of them in hospital.

THE MOST DANGEROUS PLACE ON EARTH

Rosenberg arrived in France at the worst possible time – right in the middle of the **Battle of the Somme**.[38] He missed the disastrous massacre of the first few days, but when he was sent to the trenches at the end of August 1916, the Somme was still the most dangerous place on earth. His chances of survival were very low. Even the most pro-war newspapers were beginning to admit that the number of **casualties** in France was far greater than had ever been predicted.

Rosenberg served in the trenches of the Somme for five months. He witnessed the full impact of war at close quarters. He wrote about what he saw in poems and letters, but says very little about the conditions at the front. He sometimes mentions the cold and the wet, but is only really interested in his work. "Winter is not the least of the horrors of war," he wrote to the poet Laurence Binyon towards the end of 1916, as he was freezing in the trenches. "I am determined that this war, with all its powers for devastation, shall not master my poeting; this is, if I am lucky enough to come through it all right."[39]

Spring Offensive

Rosenberg's health broke down at the beginning of 1917. For much of that year, he was in and out of hospital, suffering from bronchitis and flu. During that time, he worked furiously on poems and plays, encouraged by the recognition that his writing was getting from influential critics. However, at the end of the year he was declared fit enough to return to the front. December saw him once again in the trenches and there he remained, with occasional rests behind the lines, until his death.

On 1 April 1918, during the German **Spring Offensive**, Rosenberg was on night patrol near the town of Fampoux on the **Western Front**. He was killed at dawn, possibly by a **sniper**'s bullet, possibly in close combat. He was buried in a mass grave. In 1926, his body was discovered and identified along with 10 others from his regiment. His remains now rest in the Bailleul Road East Cemetery, Saint-Laurent-Blangy, near Arras, northern France.

> **LINK**
> The Commonwealth War Graves Commission is a searchable database of war cemeteries, including Rosenberg's burial place: www.cwgc.org

RUPERT BROOKE

Born: Rugby,
Warwickshire, 1887
Died: Skyros,
Greece, 1915

Rupert Brooke rocketed
to fame in 1915 when
his poem "The Soldier"
was read aloud in St
Paul's Cathedral, just a
few months before his
death. His work inspired
thousands of young men
to enlist.

DID YOU KNOW?
Brooke died from blood
poisoning resulting from
an infected mosquito bite.

Rupert Brooke was the pin-up boy of the war poets. He was famous for his good looks as well as his poetry before the war broke out. He became one of the most celebrated figures of his generation after his death at the age of 27.

His father, William Brooke, was a housemaster at Rugby, one of the UK's major **public schools**. Rupert was the second of three sons. He had a happy, secure childhood, and was a star athlete as well as an excellent scholar. He even won prizes for his poetry. It was obvious to everyone that Rupert would go far. "Almost everyone came under the sway of his personality,"[40] wrote his schoolfriend Hugh Russell-Smith.

In 1906, Brooke went to King's College, Cambridge, to study Classics. Here, too, he quickly attracted attention. He acted in plays and wrote poetry.

Brooke campaigned on behalf of the Labour Party and the Fabian Society, which believed in equal distribution of wealth. He was elected to the Cambridge Apostles, an influential "secret society". This brought him into contact with some of the major artists and thinkers of his generation.

Brooke spent his summer holidays touring Europe and visiting friends in London. He soon became involved with the Bloomsbury Group, a circle of artists and writers who were the major creative force in England at the time. His first book, *Poems*, was published in 1911 when he was 24. He was well on the way to becoming famous.

"DREAMS OF GLORY"

Later, Brooke suffered ill health and a series of failed relationships, which led to a breakdown in 1913. He spent much of that year travelling in North America, returning to England via Fiji and Tahiti. He got home just before the outbreak of war and **enlisted** straight away, spurred on by **patriotism**. He received a **commission** from Winston Churchill, then First Lord of the Admiralty, to the Royal Naval Division.

As early as October 1914, Brooke was sailing to Europe. He was sent to Antwerp in Belgium, where he witnessed some shelling but little in the way of direct action. "When they told us ... that we were all going to be killed in Antwerp," he wrote in a letter,[41] "I thought 'what Hell it is that I shan't have any children' ... And we were barely even under fire, in the end!"

> "A young Apollo, golden-haired,
> Stands dreaming on the verge of strife,
> Magnificently unprepared
> For the long littleness of life."
>
> *On Rupert Brooke*, Frances Cornford (1910)

LINK
Find out more about Rupert Brooke at the Poetry Foundation website: www.poetryfoundation.org/bio/rupert-brooke

Brooke must have been excited to be selected as part of the mission to the **Dardanelles** in 1915. The objective was simple: to capture the city of Constantinople (modern Istanbul) from Turkey. This would create a safe route for **Allied** ships to Russia. "It's too wonderful for belief," he wrote on hearing the news.[42] "I'm filled with confident and glorious hopes."

Dead before battle

The Dardanelles campaign was a disaster. It culminated in the Battle of **Gallipoli** (April 1915 to January 1916) with massive **casualties** on both sides. It was one of the turning points in attitudes towards the war.

Brooke never made it to the battle. On 28 February 1915, he sailed from Bristol into the Mediterranean and along the north African coast. He seemed to be in a dream world. "We've had rather a nice voyage," he wrote in March, "very smooth and delicious."[43]

Rupert Brooke's film-star good looks made him popular during his lifetime and even more famous after his death in 1915.

On 17 April, the ship landed on the Greek island of Skyros. Four days later, Brooke became ill with a temperature of 103 degrees. He was transferred to a French hospital ship moored in the Aegean Sea, but it was too late: he died of blood poisoning on 23 April.

"ENGLAND'S NOBLEST SON"

Brooke's story does not end there. Three days after his death, Winston Churchill wrote a letter to *The Times* newspaper praising Brooke's poetry and describing him as "all that one could wish England's noblest sons to be".[44] It is this image that ensured the poet's immortality.

> "During the last few months of his life ... the poet-soldier told with all the simple force of genius the sorrow of youth about to die ... He expected to die: he was willing to die for the dear England whose beauty and majesty he knew."
>
> Brooke's obituary by Winston Churchill, *The Times*, 26 April 1915[45]

MEMORIAL

Rupert Brooke was buried in a simple grave with a stone cairn and a wooden cross. Shortly after the war, his mother commissioned a more permanent grave to be built on the same site, adding an inscription from "The Soldier" to it. In 1931, a further memorial was built in Skyros Town, featuring a statue of an "ideal poet".[46]

ENGLAND DECLARES WAR ON GERMANY—
1. CHIPPING NORTON TERRITORIALS GOING ON SERVICE. AUG 5. 1914

"THE SOLDIER"

Rupert Brooke's poem "The Soldier" was published in *The Times*, where it reached a massive audience.[47] Its **romantic**, **idealized**

Early volunteers were sent off on a wave of patriotic fervour, which was depicted in Brooke's poetry. Few returned.

vision of a soldier-hero sacrificing himself for his country perfectly summed up England's mood at the time, before the true cost of the conflict was revealed. Brooke's reputation, both good and bad, rests mostly on that poem. The opening lines are far removed from the realistic poetry of Sassoon and Owen. Many have criticized Brooke for avoiding the horror of war, and for valuing patriotism and glory more than human suffering.

It is certainly true that Brooke's poetry has little in common with the mud, blood, and pain described by his **contemporaries**. But that is not to say that he was deliberately ignoring them. Brooke died in April 1915, before the disaster of Gallipoli and the massive **casualties** on the **Western Front**. He died before the hard facts of trench warfare were known. None of the other poets had written anything serious or angry by this time, either. It's possible that Brooke, had he lived, would have changed his attitude to the war. Given his left-wing politics and **pacifist** connections, it's likely that he would have become as much a critic of the war as Sassoon and Owen.

> "If I should die, think only this of me:
> That there's some corner of a foreign field
> That is for ever England. There shall be
> In that rich earth a richer dust concealed;
> A dust whom England bore, shaped, made aware"
>
> "The Soldier" (1914)

Other poetry

Brooke wrote another famous poem, "The Old Vicarage, Grantchester", in May 1912 in Berlin. He was terribly homesick and depressed and the intensity of his longing for England bursts out of every line, most famously the final couplet: "Stands the Church clock at ten to three? / And is there honey still for tea?" But alongside that sweet nostalgia, some sadness comes out in other poems – for example, "A Channel Passage" with its description of seasickness, and "The Fish", which is a **satire** on religion.

But it's "The Soldier" and the four other 1914 sonnets that make Brooke an important war poet. More than any other writer, he expressed the national feeling in the early months of World War I. His words inspired and comforted many hundreds of thousands of soldiers and their families.

DISCUSSION TOPIC

Did Brooke glorify war?
Brooke's poetry makes going to war and dying for your country sound heroic and glorious. It is a different interpretation of war from that found in Owen and Sassoon's later poetry, but does that make Brooke a worse poet? Do you think Brooke's attitude to war would have changed, like Sassoon's, if he had seen action?

LINK
You can read all of Rupert Brooke's poems online at the Rupert Brooke Society website: www.rupertbrooke.com

ROBERT GRAVES

Born: Wimbledon, London, 1895
Died: Majorca, Spain, 1985

Robert Graves was the first of the major World War I poets to publish his work. He survived the war and went on to have a hugely successful career as a poet and novelist.

DID YOU KNOW?
Graves's novel *I, Claudius* was the basis for one of the most famous TV series of the 1970s.

Of all the war poets, it is Robert Graves who went on to have the most successful career. He was one of the lucky ones: despite one very near miss, he survived the trenches. By the late 1920s, Graves was an internationally famous writer.

Robert Graves was born into a middle-class family. His mother, Amalie von Ranke, was German.[48] The worsening political situation in Europe meant that anti-German feeling was running high. Secondary school for Robert was a nightmare. He was bullied because of his mother's nationality and his own strong, artistic temperament. He became isolated and deeply unhappy. Then war was declared when Graves was 19, so he **enlisted** immediately in the Royal Welch Fusiliers.[49]

Poetic pioneer

Graves's first volume of poems, *Over the Brazier*, was published in 1916. It gained attention for its realistic tone, which was very different from the lush, sentimental style that was in fashion. In France, Graves became friends with Siegfried Sassoon, and he influenced Sassoon's writing style (see page 20).

Graves was badly wounded at the **Battle of the Somme** and spent most of the rest of the war in England and Ireland. He married Nancy Nicholson just before the **Armistice** in 1918. He took up his deferred place at Oxford University and carried on writing. He and Nancy had four children.

His first marriage ended and Graves settled on the Spanish island of Majorca. He had four more children with his second wife, Beryl Pritchard. By now he was a literary celebrity: his autobiography, *Good-Bye to All That* (1929), recounted his war experiences and his friendship with Sassoon and Owen.

Successful author

Graves never stopped writing poetry, and there's no doubt that it was his greatest love. But he is best known for his prose. In 1934, he published *I, Claudius*, a fictionalized account of the life of the Roman emperor. It was a global bestseller. His non-fiction writings on history and mythology, particularly *The Greek Myths* (1955), were also popular.

In later life, Graves suffered from memory loss. He was unable to write much after the age of 80. He survived for a further ten years, and is buried near his home on Majorca.

> "It's hard to know if you're alive or dead
> When steel and fire go roaring through your head."
>
> "It's a Queer Time" (1915)

LINK
For more on the life and work of Robert Graves, see **www.robertgraves.org**

REPORTED DEAD

Graves enlisted as a soldier in 1914 full of **patriotic** enthusiasm. He was excited to be going to war and unaware of what he would find when he got there.

 Military hospitals had to treat a wide range of injuries as well as psychological conditions. Many were basic, makeshift outfits like this one set up in a church in France, in around 1917.

It didn't take him long to find out. Graves recalled his trench experience in his post-war autobiography *Good-Bye to All That*, one of the most important records of what life was like for soldiers serving at the front. "The trench was cut through red clay," he wrote of his first day. "I had a torch with me which I kept flashed on the ground. Hundreds of field mice and frogs were in the trench. They had fallen in and had no way out. The light dazzled them and we could not help treading on them. So I put the torch back in my pocket."[50]

On 20 July 1916, just before his 21st birthday, Graves was hit by a shell **fragment**. It entered his shoulder and chest, hitting his right lung and very nearly killing him. His death was reportedly announced in *The Times* newspaper, much to the distress of his family, who only found out that he was still alive when he came back to England.

Shell shock and after

An injured lung wasn't Graves's only problem: he was suffering from **shell shock**. He made a full recovery from his physical injuries, but the **psychological** after-effects stayed with him for at least ten years.

Once he'd left hospital, Graves was eager to get back to the front. He secured a posting to France, only to be told by his company surgeon that he was not fit for action. He was sent home and threatened with a **court martial** if he disobeyed.[51]

Graves spent the rest of the war in non-combat service, mostly training troops for the front. "I thought of going back to France," he wrote, "but realised the absurdity of the notion. Since 1916, the fear of gas obsessed me: any unusual smell, even a sudden strong smell of flowers in a garden, was enough to send me trembling. And I couldn't face the sound of heavy shelling now; the noise of a car back-firing would send me flat on my face, or running for cover."[52]

W.H.R. Rivers (1864–1922) was a pioneering doctor. He was one of the first to use **psychoanalysis** to address the problems of men who had served in the trenches. Graves met Rivers when he escorted Siegfried Sassoon for treatment for shell shock at Craiglockhart War Hospital (see page 17). Graves himself was not treated by Rivers but he was interested in the doctor's ideas on the mental process of writing poetry.[53]

> "Another war soon gets begun,
> A dirtier, a more glorious one
> Then, boys, you'll have to play, all in;
> It's the cruellest team will win.
> So hold your nose against the stink
> And never stop too long to think.
> Wars don't change except in name;
> The next one must go just the same."

"The Next War" (1917)

REPORTING FROM THE FRONT

Graves was the first British war poet to write about his experiences in direct, sometimes brutal language without any flowery "poetic" touches. His book *Over the Brazier* contains work he mostly wrote at the front. It is a stark contrast to the work of Rupert Brooke. It is written in everyday language that other soldiers would understand, and it doesn't avoid unpleasant realities. Little wonder that Siegfried Sassoon, who was serving in the same battalion, was so influenced by Graves's work.

Graves knew that what he was doing was different. In 1940, he wrote an article about the poetry of World War I that described the work of Rupert Brooke and other early war poets as "gallant and **idealistic** but with hardly a real poet among them".[54] The change, he said, came in 1917 with the realization that too many people were dying for no good reason. This was exactly when Sassoon and Owen started writing their best work.

Graves was being modest: he'd already got there two years earlier. In July 1915, he wrote one of his best-known poems, "A Dead Boche". It describes his discovery of a corpse in a wood. (*Boche* is a slang word for "German".) "Propped up against a shattered trunk, / In a great mess of things unclean, / Sat a dead Boche ... Dribbling black blood from nose and beard."

MOVING ON FROM WAR

Most of Graves's war poetry was published in the three volumes *Over the Brazier* and *Goliath and David* (1916), and *Fairies and Fusiliers* (1917). He returned to the subject often in later life, as he struggled to come to terms with what had happened to him. But it is his war poems that built his reputation.

Graves's work is not always easy to read. It is nowhere near as emotional or angry as that of Owen and Sassoon, which explains why it's not so famous. Unlike Sassoon, Graves managed to move on from the war and find new, bigger subjects to write about. He was thinking, perhaps, of some of his fellow poets when he wrote the bittersweet poem "When I'm Killed". "So when I'm killed, don't wait for me ... You'll find me buried, living-dead / In these verses that you've read."

Robert Graves was one of Britain's most successful authors by the time this photo was taken, in 1941.

LINK
Read more of Graves's wartime experiences in extracts from his 1929 autobiography *Good-Bye to All That* at **projects.oucs.ox.ac.uk/jtap/rose/goodbye.html**

DISCUSSION TOPIC

Stark language
Why did Robert Graves decide to write about the war in such simple, straightforward language? And why was this such a big influence on other poets?

39

VERA BRITTAIN

Born: Buxton, Derbyshire, 1893
Died: Wimbledon, London, 1970

Vera Brittain was one of the outstanding female poets of World War I. She served as a nurse in a hospital on the Western Front.

DID YOU KNOW?
Brittain's book *Testament of Youth*, about her wartime experiences, was adapted for television in 1979. It has since been made into a feature film.

Vera Brittain[55] was the daughter of a wealthy paper mill owner. She dreamed of being a writer from an early age. When war was declared, she had a place at Oxford University, but she decided to become a nurse instead. Most of her fellow students, as well as her brother and her fiancé, had **enlisted**, and Brittain felt she couldn't stay at home. She joined the Voluntary Aid Detachment (VAD), which was set up to assist professional nurses in the event of a war. She trained first at Buxton and then in London.

In 1916, Brittain was posted to a hospital in Malta, and in August 1917, she was sent to the military hospital at Étaples in France, close to the **Western Front**. In her first month at Étaples, nearly 35,000 wounded soldiers were admitted to the hospital – an average of more than a thousand a day.

The hospital admitted anyone, no matter which side they were fighting on, so at first she worked on the German ward. It was while Brittain was looking after enemy soldiers that she began to realize that the war was not a simple question of right against wrong. It was a much deeper tragedy of human suffering.

Brittain had other reasons to grieve: in 1915, her fiancé Roland Leighton was killed; then, in 1918, her brother Edward. She also lost several other close friends. It was this tragedy, both personal and universal, that inspired Brittain's writing.

TESTAMENT OF YOUTH

Brittain's early poetry recorded what she saw on the wards. *Verses of a VAD* was published just before the end of the war. She dedicated the book to her late fiancé, Roland Leighton.

After the war, Brittain returned to England and carried on working as a nurse before taking up her place at Oxford in 1919. After graduating, she moved to London and started writing fiction. In 1933, nearly 20 years after the war, she wrote the first volume of her autobiography. *Testament of Youth* detailed her experiences as a nurse. It became a global bestseller, and Brittain had a successful career that lasted until her death in 1970. She continued to campaign for the cause that was closest to her heart: **pacifism**.

"When I think of [my brother] Edward in one part of France working to annihilate these very same people that I in another part am working to save, I begin to realise the folly and tragedy of war in a way I never did before."

Vera Brittain on nursing German **casualties**, from a 1917 article[56]

LINK

Read more about Vera Brittain's life and work at **www.spartacus.schoolnet. co.uk/Jbrittain.htm**

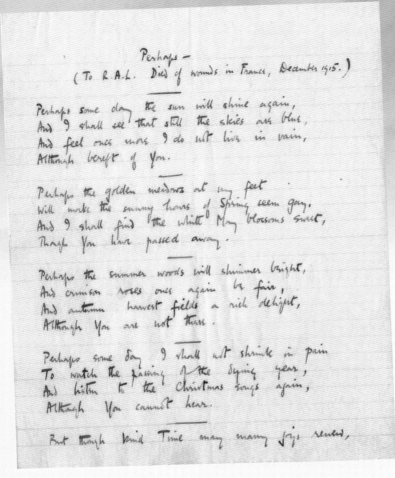

Perhaps —
(To R.A.L. Died of wounds in France, December 1915.)

Perhaps some day the sun will shine again,
And I shall see that still the skies are blue,
And feel once more I do not live in vain,
Although bereft of You.

Perhaps the golden meadows at my feet
Will make the sunny hours of Spring seem gay,
And I shall find the white May blossoms sweet,
Though You have passed away.

Perhaps the summer woods will shimmer bright,
And crimson roses once again be fair,
And autumn harvest fields a rich delight,
Although You are not there.

Perhaps some day I shall not shrink in pain
To watch the passing of the dying year,
And listen to the Christmas songs again,
Although You cannot hear.

But though kind Time may many joys renew,

The manuscript of "Perhaps", Vera Brittain's moving farewell to her fiancé Roland Leighton, who was killed in 1915.

"LOVE AMIDST WAR"

Brittain's early poetry was written from the point of view of a young woman watching her brother, fiancé, and male friends going off to fight. She was still, by her own admission, under the influence of Rupert Brooke,[57] and she saw something **romantic** and heroic about the beginning of the conflict. The reality of war hit her quickly and hard. In 1916, she wrote the moving "Perhaps". It was a painful farewell to her dead fiancé. "Perhaps some day the sun will shine again," she writes.

The tone of Brittain's poetry changed when she started nursing at Étaples. First, her poems were composed quickly during rare moments of rest. She sent them back to her family without much polishing.

Second, Brittain was writing about the real consequences of war, and her personal reactions to it. "Never … have I seen such dreadful wounds," she wrote in 1917.[58] "It gives one a chance to live up to our Motto 'Inter arma caritas'." This was the Red Cross motto ("Love amidst war"). Brittain used it as the subtitle for her first great poem "The German Ward", which she wrote at Étaples. "The German Ward" is a completely different poem from anything she'd written before. She reports on conditions in the ward – "the bitter groans and laboured breath … and sights and smells of blood and wounds and death". It was as simple and harrowing as Owen's work of the same period.

REMEMBERING THE DEAD

In June 1918, Brittain wrote "To My Brother" to commemorate her brother Edward's bravery at the **Battle of the Somme** in 1916. "Your battle-wounds are scars upon my heart, / Received when in that grand and tragic '**show**' / You played your part / Two years ago." Brittain sent the poem to Edward, then serving in Italy – but it arrived too late. He was killed in action just four days after she wrote it.

She returned to the subject of Edward's death, and that of Roland Leighton, time and time again, struggling to deal with the many losses she suffered in a few short years.

DISCUSSION TOPIC

Female war poet
Vera Brittain was one of the few female war poets whose work was well known at the time. Are there any qualities to her work that make it different from the poetry of male writers?

LINK
Read more of Vera Brittain's poems at the First World War Digital Poetry Archive: www.oucs.ox.ac.uk/ww1lit/collections/brittain

"After seeing some of the dreadful things I have to see here, I feel I shall never be the same person again, and wonder if, when the war does end, I shall have forgotten how to laugh."

Letter from Vera Brittain to Roland Leighton (1915)[59]

CHARLES SORLEY

Born: Aberdeen, Scotland, 1895
Died: Loos, France, 1915

Charles Sorley was only 20 when he died in the trenches, but many consider him to be one of the most talented war poets.

DID YOU KNOW?
Sorley was one of the few poets who expressed serious sympathy with the German enemy.

Charles Hamilton Sorley was the son of a university professor who moved the family from Aberdeen to Cambridge when Charles was five.[60] Charles started writing in his teens, submitting poems to the school magazine. He also played football and his favourite pastime was running in the countryside. His love of the natural world and history are qualities that stand out in his early work.

After leaving school, Sorley spent a few months travelling around Europe before starting at university. A trip to Germany, where he stayed for just over seven months, was the turning point in his life. He loved every minute of the trip – and he particularly loved the German people. "I felt I was a German," he wrote in February 1914, "and proud to be a German ... I felt that perhaps I could die for Deutschland – and I have never had an inkling of that feeling about England, and never shall." [61]

WAR ARRIVES

Blissfully unaware of the gathering storm, Sorley set off on a walking tour of the Moselle Valley in July. On 2 August, a couple of days before Britain declared war on Germany, he and his friend were arrested as English spies. They spent a night in prison before returning, hurriedly, to England. Sorley applied for a **commission** to become an officer, and within a few days was accepted as a second lieutenant in the Suffolk Regiment. Even then, he was uncertain about the rights and wrongs of the war. "I regard the war as one between sisters," he wrote in a letter of October 1914, "the efficient and intolerant against the casual and sympathetic."[62]

"Germany's only fault ... is a lack of real insight and sympathy with those who differ from her. We are not fighting a bully, but a **bigot**."

Letter from Charles Sorley to his friend A.J. Hopkinson (1914)[63]

Early death

By the time Sorley's battalion was sent to France in May 1915, his attitude to the war was hardening. A quick encounter with death, when one of his men accidentally blew himself up with a bomb, made Sorley realize the muddle and mess of the fight.

In August 1915, he was promoted to the rank of captain and his leave was cancelled. At the outbreak of the Battle of Loos on the **Western Front**, he led his company to the front line, where he was killed by a **sniper**'s bullet in the trenches. He was only 20 years old.

LINK

Find out more about Sorley's life and work at www.firstworldwar.com/poetsandprose/sorley.htm

"YOU ARE BLIND LIKE US"

Sorley only wrote 37 complete poems[64] before he died. But such was his talent that Robert Graves considered him to be "one of the three poets of importance killed during the war",[65] the other two being Wilfred Owen and Isaac Rosenberg.

What makes Sorley special is his balanced attitude towards the rights and wrongs of World War I. His life in Germany just before the war made him sympathetic to his European neighbours. He also had little faith in Britain's moral rightness – he joined up, he said, "in a spirit of dutiful but unenthusiastic **patriotism**". From the start, he saw the war as a total tragedy rather than a simple battle between good and evil. In one of his most famous poems, "To Germany", written in 1914, he says, "In each other's dearest ways we stand, / And hiss and hate. And the blind fight the blind."

> "You are blind like us. Your hurt no man designed,
> And no man claimed the conquest of your land.
> But gropers both through fields of thought confined
> We stumble and we do not understand."
>
> "To Germany" (1914)

 British troops advance to attack through a cloud of **poison gas,** as viewed from the trench which they have just left. This remarkable snapshot was taken by a soldier of the London Rifle Brigade on the opening day of the Battle of Loos, 25 September 1915.

The final poem

Sorley's two most famous poems take very different attitudes towards the war. "All the Hills and Vales Along" was written at about the same time as "To Germany". Like Brooke's "The Soldier", it is about young men marching off to battle. But unlike Brooke, who saw glory in the coming danger, Sorley saw only death. "All the hills and vales along / Earth is bursting into song, / And the singers are the chaps / Who are going to die perhaps." The only comfort for Sorley, that great lover of nature and history, is that death would reunite men with the earth.

Sorley's poems questioned the popular view of the Germans as cruel monsters, as depicted here in a wartime cartoon "The Gentle German".

Sorley's last poem was found in his kit after he died,[66] and sent home to his parents with his other possessions. It must have been hard for them to read. "When you see millions of the mouthless dead / Give them not praise. For, deaf, how should they know / It is not curses heaped on each gashed head?". Perhaps this is the poem that gives us the best idea of what Sorley might have been capable of if he'd lived.

DISCUSSION TOPIC

A sympathetic attitude
Sorley believed that both Britain and Germany were wrong to go to war. How does his attitude differ from that of other poets? Did it affect his work?

LINK
Read more about Sorley's work at www.poemhunter.com/charles-hamilton-sorley

ALAN SEEGER

Born: New York City, New York, USA, 1888
Died: Belloy-en-Santerre, France, 1916

Alan Seeger was an American citizen living in Paris in 1914. He volunteered for the French Foreign Legion and fought for France.

DID YOU KNOW?
His nephew, Pete Seeger (born 1919), is a famous American folk singer and songwriter.

Alan Seeger grew up in New York and Mexico. He attended the élite US university Harvard, where he was friends with the poet T.S. Eliot. He then spent some years drifting between the United States and France, trying to become a writer. In 1912, he moved to Paris. He loved the city, and wrote a great deal of very enthusiastic verse about it, but none of it compares to his later work.

When war was declared in August 1914, Seeger could easily have returned home – the United States didn't enter the war until 1917, so there was no need for him to fight. But out of solidarity with his French friends, he volunteered for the French Foreign Legion, which is made up of people from foreign countries who want to fight for France. He went straight into training in Toulouse.

Soon Seeger was in the trenches, where he spent the winter of 1914 and much of 1915. The experience was a stark contrast to the noble impulse that inspired him to **enlist** in the first place. "You must not be anxious about my not coming back," he wrote to his mother in June 1915. "The chances are about ten to one that I will. But if I should not, you must be proud ... I could not have done otherwise than I did, and I think I could not have done better. Death is nothing terrible after all." [67]

"Whether I am on the winning or losing side is not the point with me: it is being on the side where my sympathies lie that matters, and I am ready to see it through to the end."

Letter from Alan Seeger to his mother, 3 July 1915[68]

LINK

Find out more about Alan Seeger at www.english.emory.edu/LostPoets/Seeger.html

FIGHTING FOR FRANCE

After many months of active service, including the Battle of Champagne, Seeger's regiment was taken off the front line. The poet spent some time in hospital, recovering from his battle experiences. In May 1916, he returned to the Somme, and in July was involved in fighting around the village of Belloy-en-Santerre. Seeger was among the first line of soldiers sent in to clear German troops from the village, and he was wounded by German machine gun fire. As he lay dying, Seeger was heard cheering on the second wave of advance, which was successful in capturing Belloy.

Seeger's poetry was published in 1917, but was not successful at the time. Over the years, however, his work has become extremely popular. Seeger is among the foreign soldiers honoured by a monument at the Place des États-Unis (United States Place) in Paris.

"THAT RARE PRIVILEGE OF DYING WELL"

Seeger, like Rupert Brooke, died relatively early in the war, before disillusionment with the slaughter had set in. His poetry celebrates the excitement and glory of war, not the brutality and **carnage**. His first war poems expressed the **idealistic** views that made him enlist with the Foreign Legion. "I found for all dear things I forfeited / A recompense ... More than dull Peace or its poor votaries could, / Taught us the dignity of being men."[69]

Even after Seeger had seen action in the trenches, particularly at the Battle of Champagne, he was obsessed by war as a glorious opportunity. He continued to see a good, early death as preferable to a long, dull life. He best summed up his feelings in his poem "Ode in Memory of the American Volunteers Fallen for France":

> "France, to you they rendered thanks
> (Seeing they came for honor, not for gain),
> Who, opening to them your glorious ranks,
> Gave them that grand occasion to excel,
> That chance to live the life most free from stain
> And that rare privilege of dying well."

Seeger died just before this sentiment of fighting for honour fell out of favour. By the time his poems were published in 1917, attitudes towards the war had changed completely, and he was quickly forgotten. His old college friend T.S. Eliot reviewed Seeger's book *Poems* in 1917. He said "Seeger was serious about his work ... It is high-flown, heavily decorated and solemn. Alan Seeger ... lived his whole life on this plane."[70]

DISCUSSION TOPIC

The "American Rupert Brooke"?
Robert Graves called Seeger an "American Rupert Brooke".[71] Is this a fair comparison? What are the main differences between Seeger and Brooke?

LINK
Read Seeger's poetry at www.poemhunter.com/alan-seeger

Seeger's reputation

Since then, Seeger has become more famous in death than he ever was in life. The poem "I Have a Rendezvous with Death" was a favourite of US President John F. Kennedy's,[72] and has become a fixture in anthologies of American poetry. Like all Seeger's poetry, it is a highly **romantic** approach to the subject. It is far removed from the realism of Graves, Sassoon, and Owen. For Seeger, death will come in spring, "when apple-blossoms fill the air … at midnight in some flaming town … I shall not fail that rendezvous." These were the words of a man who still believed that death in battle was glorious, who regarded war as "the majesty of strife".[73] He died still believing in these ideals.

> "If it must be, let it come in the heat of action. Why flinch? It is by far the noblest form in which death can come. It is in a sense almost a privilege."
>
> Letter from Alan Seeger to *The New York Sun*, 22 May 1915[74]

Monument to the American volunteers who fought for France, Place des États-Unis, Paris. Seeger's poetry is engraved around the base.

OTHER VOICES

Hundreds of poets from many countries wrote about World War I. Some of them became famous, while some wrote only a couple of significant works. Some survived the war, but many died in the trenches. Their work, and their life stories, give us great insight into the events of 1914 to 1918 – not just from the point of view of the **Allies**, but also from the "enemy", Germany.

EDMOND ADAM (1889–1918)

Edmond Adam was a civil engineer who volunteered for active service in 1914. He fought right through the war until his death in August 1918. Very little is known of Adam's life, but he started contributing poems to the anti-war magazine *Les Humbles* in 1918. This included his best-known work "Coqs de Combat", which shocked with its direct, violent language.

TRY READING: "Coqs de Combat" (or "Gamecocks")

LAURENCE BINYON (1869–1943)

Laurence Binyon was too old to **enlist** as a soldier, but volunteered as a hospital orderly in France, tending to the wounded from Verdun. After the war, he resumed his job at the British Museum in London, where he became an internationally famous art expert. His poem "For the Fallen", written in 1914 after the Battle of the Marne, has become one of the most famous war poems of all time. It is often read out at **Remembrance Sunday** services.

TRY READING: "For the Fallen"

EDMUND BLUNDEN (1896–1974)

Edmund Blunden was **commissioned** as an officer in 1915 at the age of just 19. He survived two solid years at the front, including at Ypres and the Somme, without serious physical injury. He wrote a great deal of poetry during and after the war. His poems were not as graphic as those of his friend Siegfried Sassoon, but they often dealt with the **psychological** effects of the experience in a profound and moving way.

TRY READING: "1916 Seen from 1921"

MARGARET POSTGATE COLE (1893–1980)

At the beginning of the war, Margaret Cole's brother was imprisoned as a **conscientious objector**. This inspired her to campaign against conscription (forcing people by law to join the army) and for **pacifism**. Her war poems express her outrage at the violence of the war and the waste of young men's lives. After the war, Cole wrote a lot on history and politics. She also wrote many detective novels with her husband, George Cole.

TRY READING: "The Veteran"

IVOR GURNEY (1890–1937)

A gifted composer, Ivor Gurney was studying at the Royal College of Music in London when war was declared. He enlisted in 1915, and wrote a good deal of poetry while serving in France. In 1917, he was wounded and gassed in France. He returned to England to recover. After the war, Gurney suffered a serious breakdown and spent much of the rest of his life in psychiatric hospitals. He continued to write poetry and music.

TRY READING: "Strange Hells"

ERNEST HEMINGWAY (1899–1961)

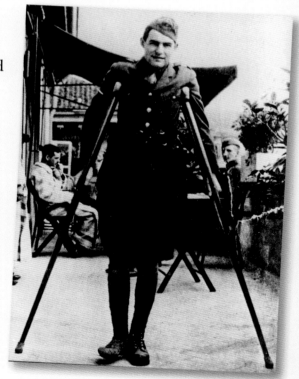

Hemingway (right) is remembered today as one of the most famous American novelists of the 20th century. At the age of 18, in 1918, he spent two months driving ambulances on the Italian front, before being badly wounded by shrapnel and sent to hospital. He remembered his wartime experiences in poems that were written in the 1920s, as he was starting his career as a writer.

TRY READING: "Killed Piave – July 8 – 1918"

RUDYARD KIPLING (1865–1936)

Rudyard Kipling was already one of Britain's most famous writers when war was declared. (He wrote *The Jungle Book* in 1894.) Being too old to fight himself, he encouraged his son John to enlist. In 1915, John was killed at the Battle of Loos, aged 18. Kipling was overwhelmed by grief and guilt, which he expressed in his poetry. It is a rare poetic response to the war from a bereaved parent.

TRY READING: "My Boy Jack"

ARCHIBALD MacLEISH (1892–1982)

Archibald MacLeish was a student at Harvard Law School when the United States entered the war. He served as an ambulance driver and later in the artillery at the second Battle of the Marne. He started writing poetry during the war, which he survived. His brother, Kenneth, did not. Some of his best poetry is about his brother's death. After the war, MacLeish rose to the office of Librarian of Congress, assistant Secretary of State, and co-founder of the United Nations Educational, Scientific, and Cultural Organization (UNESCO).

TRY READING: "The Silent Slain"

BENJAMIN PÉRET (1899–1959)

Benjamin Péret served with the French army in the Balkans and Greece. He started writing poetry during this time. After the war, Péret became one of the leading poets of anti-war artistic movements in France. He published his first volume of poetry in 1921. He later fought in the Spanish Civil War, and emigrated to Mexico.

TRY READING: "Petite Chanson des Mutilés" (or "Little Song of the Maimed")

HERBERT READ (1893–1968)

Herbert Read was a student at the University of Leeds when war was declared. He served in France, received the **Military Cross** and the Distinguished Service Order, and reached the rank of captain. Most of his war poetry was published in his second book, *Naked Warriors* (1919). After the war, Read became an art critic and a supporter of anarchism, where individuals enjoy freedom without government.

TRY READING: "Meditation of a Dying German Officer"

EDWARD THOMAS (1878–1917)

Edward Thomas (right) was already an established poet when the war started. He was celebrated for his portraits of nature and traditional English landscapes, especially in his famous poem "Adlestrop". Despite his age and his young family, Thomas enlisted in 1915. He arrived in France as a second lieutenant in 1917 but was killed shortly afterwards, at the Battle of Arras. His war poetry is remarkable for its focus on the natural world.

TRY READING: "In Memoriam (Easter 1915)"

ERNST STADLER (1883–1914)

Born in Alsace-Lorraine, now part of Germany, Ernst Stadler studied for a while at Oxford University before returning home and becoming a poet. He was influenced by the philosopher Nietzsche, and he believed war was a necessary crisis to renew Europe. He went off to fight in 1914 full of hope and excitement. He was killed by a British grenade a few weeks later.

TRY READING: "Der Aufbruch" (or "Setting Out")

AUGUST STRAMM (1874–1915)

August Stramm was a central figure in the circle of Berlin artists known as the Expressionists. Today, he is best known as a playwright. His poetry, like his plays, is tense, violent, and **fragmented**. It captures some of the fear and panic as well as the excitement that greeted the outbreak of war in Germany. Stramm served as an officer in France and on the Eastern Front, where he died in hand-to-hand combat.

TRY READING: "Wunde" (or "Wound")

TIMELINE

World War I was a global war centred in Europe. It began on 28 July 1914 and lasted until 11 November 1918. At the time, it was known as the Great War, but then became known as World War I after there had been a second world war, from 1939 to 1945.

1914: OPENING MOVES

WAR DECLARED
HOPES OF QUICK RESULTS FADE – STALEMATE AND TRENCH WARFARE

28 June	Archduke Ferdinand of Austria is assassinated in Sarajevo by Serbian nationalist Gavrilo Princip
28 July	Austria-Hungary declares war on Serbia
1 August	Outbreak of war: Germany declares war on Russia
3 August	Germany declares war on France
4 August	Germany invades Belgium. Britain declares war on Germany. President Woodrow Wilson declares US **neutrality**.
26 August	Start of the Battle of Tannenberg, Germany's biggest success of the war on the Eastern Front (which was in Russia)
5 September	Start of the first Battle of the Marne, which halted the German advance into France and resulted in stalemate and trench warfare
14 October	Start of the first Battle of Ypres, an attempt by both sides to bring the war to a swift conclusion. After weeks of fighting in Belgium and huge losses, neither side had gained the advantage.
29 October	Turkey enters the war
30 October	Poet Ernst Stadler dies
21 December	First German air raid on Britain
25 December	Unofficial Christmas truce is declared by troops on the **Western Front**

1915: STALEMATE IN THE TRENCHES

ALLIES FAIL TO STOP GERMAN ADVANCES ON WESTERN FRONT – GERMANS ALSO SUCCESSFUL IN EAST – MASSACRE AT GALLIPOLI

4 February	German **U-boat** attacks ships in an attempt to cut off supplies to Britain
19 February	Beginning of **Allied** land and sea action on the **Dardanelles** and **Gallipoli**, Turkey, which results in Turkish siege of Allied forces
4 April	Rupert Brooke's "The Soldier" is read out in St Paul's Cathedral
22 April	Start of the second Battle of Ypres with the first use of **poison gas** by Germans
23 April	Poet Rupert Brooke dies
25 April	Allied landings at Gallipoli
7 May	Sinking of British passenger liner *Lusitania* by a German U-boat off the Irish coast, with several American **casualties**. The event threatens US neutrality.
1 September	Poet August Stramm dies
25 September	Opening of the second Battle of Champagne, an unsuccessful French attempt to halt German invasion. This sets the scene for the 1916 Battle of Verdun.
13 October	Poet Charles Sorley dies
19 December	Field Marshal Douglas Haig becomes Commander-in-Chief of the troops that were sent to the Western Front
28 December	Withdrawal of Allied troops from Gallipoli begins

MASSIVE BATTLES AT SOMME AND VERDUN KILL HUNDREDS OF THOUSANDS

– *No Decisive Victory in France – Biggest Ever Naval Battle at Jutland*

Publication of Robert Graves's first volume of war poetry, *Over the Brazier*

21 February	Start of Battle of Verdun as Germany attempts to secure stranglehold on France. This leads to the longest battle of the war.
24 April	Beginning of Easter Rising against British rule in Ireland
27 April	Field Marshal Lord Kitchener, British Secretary of State for War, asks for military assistance from the United States, which is still neutral
31 May–1 June	Battle of Jutland, the biggest naval battle in history, off the coast of Denmark: 14 British and 11 German ships sunk, with no decisive outcome
1 July	Start of the **Battle of the Somme**. The British Army suffers nearly 60,000 casualties on the first day.
4 July	Poet Alan Seeger dies
September	Publication of *Soldier Poets: Songs of the Fighting Men*, an influential anthology of war poetry that sells well in the United States
15 September	First use of tanks by the British, on the Somme battlefield
18 November	End of the Battle of the Somme, with small advances made by the Allies
28 November	First German aeroplane raid on London
5 December	Asquith resigns as Prime Minister, and is replaced by David Lloyd George

U-BOAT CAMPAIGN BRINGS U.S. INTO THE WAR

Russian Revolution – Deadlock on Western Front

Publication of Graves's *Fairies and Fusiliers*

9 January	Germany launches policy of unrestricted U-boat warfare
February	Strikes and protests mark start of **Russian Revolution**
3 February	US severs relations with Germany
23 February	German tactical withdrawal to defensible positions on Hindenburg Line in north-eastern France
15 March	Tsar Nicholas II of Russia abdicates
6 April	US declares war on Germany
9 April	Start of Nivelle Offensive, another unsuccessful French attempt to repel German invasion, with costly battles at Aisne and Champagne. Poet Edward Thomas dies.
May	Publication of Siegfried Sassoon's first collection of war poetry, *The Old Huntsman*
26 June	First US troops arrive in France
6 July	T.E. Lawrence (known as Lawrence of Arabia) captures territory from Turks in the Arab Revolt
16 July	Passchendaele offensive begins in Flanders, an Allied attempt to push Germans out of Belgium
30 July	Sassoon's "Finished with the War" is read to the House of Commons
31 July	Major British offensive at third Battle of Ypres
August	Wilfred Owen and Sassoon meet in Craiglockhart War Hospital, Edinburgh
4 August	Vera Brittain starts work at Étaples Hospital on the Western Front
1 September	Riga Offensive marks further German success on the Eastern Front
7 November	Start of "October Revolution" marks decisive phase of Russian Revolution and beginning of Russian Civil War as Lenin takes control
20 November	British launch surprise attack at Cambrai in France, breaking through the Hindenburg Line

GERMAN SPRING OFFENSIVE NEARLY DEFEATS ALLIES

ALLIED COUNTER-ATTACK TURNS THE TABLES
HINDENBURG LINE BREACHED – ARMISTICE

January	Russia leaves the war
21 March	Germany launches the **Spring Offensive**, the first of five assaults against the Allied forces, starting with the Battle of Picardy, taking back much of the Somme. The fighting now becomes more fluid, not tied to the front lines that had existed for the previous three years.
1 April	Poet Isaac Rosenberg dies
9 April	Germans launch second phase of their offensive at Battle of the Lys, leading to significant gains in Flanders and the near collapse of the Allied armies in Europe
25 May	German U-boats appear in US waters
27 May	Third phase of German offensive begins at the third Battle of the Aisne
9 June	Opening of the fourth phase of German offensive (Battle of the Matz)
July	Publication of Sassoon's *Counter-Attack*
15 July	Final phase of German offensive (second Battle of the Marne) leads to German defeat and decisive turning of tide in favour of Allies
16–17 July	Murder of Tsar Nicholas II and his family in Russia
18 July	Start of Allied counter-attack, seizing strategical initiative from Germans
8 August	Start of Battle of Amiens marks the beginning of the Allied "Hundred Days Offensive", forcing German troops back to the Hindenburg Line
24 August	Poet Edmond Adam dies
27 September	First major breaches of Hindenburg Line by Allied forces
3–4 October	Germans and Austrians send notes to US President Woodrow Wilson requesting an **armistice**
8 October	Start of decisive Battle of Cambrai leads to speedy Allied victory
21 October	Germany calls off U-boat campaign
30 October	Turkey agrees to armistice with Allies
3 November	German Navy mutinies at Kiel
4 November	Poet Wilfred Owen dies
7 November	Germany enters armistice negotiations
9 November	Kaiser Wilhelm II abdicates
11 November	Armistice goes into effect as fighting ceases at 11 a.m.

1919: AFTERMATH

PEACE CONFERENCE
— THE TREATY OF VERSAILLES

10 January	Start of communist revolt in Berlin
18 January	Peace negotiations open in Paris
25 January	Peace conference accepts principle of a League of Nations
21 June	German fleet scuttled (sinks itself) at Scapa Flow
28 June	Treaty of Versailles signed in the Hall of Mirrors at Versailles
19 July	Cenotaph (monument to the war dead) is unveiled in London

FIND OUT MORE

World War I has been inspiring artists, writers, and film makers for a hundred years. Poetry is one of the most important ways in which we can find out about what it was like to live through the war, but here are some other suggestions.

NON-FICTION BOOKS

If You're Reading This... Last Letters from the Front Line, Sian Price (Frontline, 2011) – Stories of soldiers serving in World War I as told by the letters they wrote home.

Letters from a Lost Generation, Vera Brittain and friends (Virago, 2008) – The correspondence between Brittain, her brother, her fiancé, and her friends gives an intimate picture of what it was like for young people living through the war.

Living Through World War I, Nicola Barber (Raintree, 2012) – How did the war affect people's everyday lives? Find out more in this survey of battles in Europe and on the home front.

NOVELS

A Farewell to Arms, Ernest Hemingway – The great American novelist used his own experience of serving in Italy during World War I to create a powerful story of the relationship between an American soldier and a British nurse.

All Quiet on the Western Front, Erich-Maria Remarque – One of the classic war novels, written in 1929 by a German veteran, it tells the story of life in the trenches. It has been filmed twice, in 1930 and 1979.

Birdsong, Sebastian Faulks – This is a moving account of a young English soldier's experience of World War I, later made into a film (2012) starring Eddie Redmayne.

War Horse, Michael Morpurgo – This is the story of Joey, a horse sent to serve on the Western Front, and the attempts of his owner Albert to get him home alive. It was made into a successful play and then a film, which was directed by Steven Spielberg.

PLAYS

Journey's End, R.C. Sherriff – First performed in London in 1928, Sherriff's play has become one of the most famous depictions of life in the trenches.

My Boy Jack, David Haig – This play is based on the true story of the famous writer Rudyard Kipling, who lost his son in World War I. A television adaptation starring Daniel Radcliffe was made in 2007.

Oh, What a Lovely War!, Joan Littlewood and others – This is a controversial musical first performed in 1963 (and filmed in 1969). It used popular wartime songs to present a highly satirical picture of how World War I was conducted.

GLOSSARY

Allies, Allied Powers Britain, France, Russia, Italy (from 1915), and the United States (from 1917), the group of countries which fought against the Central Powers (Germany, Austria-Hungary, the Ottoman Empire under Turkish rule, Bulgaria) in World War I. Other nations were also involved on both sides.

armistice truce. An armistice was signed between the Allies and Germany to cease all fighting on the Western Front during World War I. It took effect on 11 November at 11 a.m. – the "eleventh hour of the eleventh day of the eleventh month" of 1918. We still remember the fallen at the same time every year.

bantam small but tough variety of poultry

Battle of the Somme one of the bloodiest battles of the war. It claimed hundreds of thousands of casualties for an overall Allied advance of 8 kilometres (5 miles). It lasted over five months, from 1 July to 18 November 1916.

bigot person who insists on believing on one set of ideas despite any evidence to the contrary

British Empire countries ruled by Britain from the 17th to the 20th century. By 1914, it was the biggest empire the world had ever seen.

carnage mass slaughter

casualty wounded or injured person

commissioned given official command over people in lower ranks in the army, air force, or navy

conscientious objector someone who refuses to fight because he or she believes that war is wrong. Conscientious objectors during World War I ("conchies") were regarded as cowards, and usually sent to prison.

contemporaries people existing at the same time, usually roughly the same age as each other

court martial trial held by army, navy, or air force to decide whether someone has broken military law. To be court-martialled is to be sent to trial.

Dardanelles long, narrow strip of sea in Turkey. It is important because it allows ships to get from the Mediterranean to the Black Sea. It was the scene of one of the most important battles of World War I.

enlist sign up or volunteer to join the army, navy, or air force

fragment small part of something, like an exploding shell. It is also used to describe a small section of a poem, sometimes an unfinished work.

Gallipoli peninsula on the western shore of the Dardanelles

idealistic believing more in ideals than reality. The idealistic approach to the war stressed duty, honour, and glory rather than death and injury.

Jewish immigrant Jewish person who leaves his or her home country to settle in another country

Military Cross one of the highest awards for bravery in the British Army

neutrality not fighting for either side in a war. The United States was neutral in World War I until 1917.

no man's land area of land between two opposing armies that is not controlled by either army

over the top when soldiers came out of their trenches and started advancing towards the enemy over exposed ground, usually under heavy fire

pacifism belief that war is always wrong, and that peace should be maintained at any price

patriotism deep and unquestioning love of one's country, and a willingness to do anything for it

poison gas type of chemical weapon. Poison gases were supposed to be illegal, but were frequently used by both sides in World War I. Mustard gas and chlorine gas were two of the most common. They burn the skin, lungs, and eyes, often with fatal results.

preface introduction – for example, to a collection of poetry – in which the author says a few words about what he or she is trying to achieve

psychoanalysis way of helping people with mental or emotional problems, encouraging patients to talk about their fears as a way of understanding them. The method was still regarded as quite new during World War I.

psychological relating to the mental and emotional state of a person

public school in the UK, a private, fee-paying school. At the time of World War I, most boys from upper class families would go to public school.

Remembrance Sunday in the UK, the Sunday in November that is nearest to 11 November, or Armistice Day

romantic in literature, something that expresses a belief in ideals, courage, and beauty. It is not just to do with love or relationships.

Russian Revolution series of political upheavals in 1917 that turned Russia from a royal society under the rule of the tsar to a Soviet Republic

satire, satirical form of writing or other expression that uses humour to expose stupidity or evil

shell shock after-effects of trench warfare, with its constant danger, explosions, and death. It caused many soldiers to experience terrible nightmares and depression. It was also known as neurasthenia. Today, we call it post-traumatic stress disorder.

show slang term used by soldiers for a battle

sniper gunman, often located at some distance from his target, relying on good aim

Spring Offensive series of military campaigns staged in 1918 by the Germans, who were trying to win the war in France

U-boat German submarine, used to devastating effect on Allied shipping; from the German *Unterseeboot* (literally, "under-sea boat")

Western Front major war zone in north-east France and Belgium. It marked the boundary between invading German forces who were pushing west, and the Allied forces who were trying to push them back.

Notes on sources

1   Tim Cross (ed.), *The Lost Voices of World War I* (Bloomsbury, 1988), p. 37
2   www.parliament.uk/documents/commons/lib/research/rp99/rp99-111.pdf
3   www.ons.gov.uk/ons/guide-method/census/2011/uk-census/index.html
4   www.parliament.uk/documents/commons/lib/research/rp99/rp99-111.pdf
5   esa.un.org/wpp/Documentation/pdf/WPP2010_Highlights.pdf
6   www.bbc.co.uk/history/british/britain_wwone/women_employment_01. shtml
7   Female workforce figures from www.economist.com/node/15174418
8   uk.answers.yahoo.com/question/index?qid=20090913104918AAInRuO
9   www.mirror.co.uk/money/personal-finance/average-family-is-over-thousand-pounds-1263319
10 Biographical details from Dominic Hibberd (ed.), *Wilfred Owen: War Poems and Others* (Chatto & Windus, 1973)
11 Ibid., p. 59
12 Ibid.
13 Ibid., p. 68
14 Ibid., pp. 61–62
15 Ibid., p. 101
16 Letter to Leslie Gunston, 22 August 1917, in Hibberd, *Wilfred Owen*, p. 73
17 Jean Moorcroft Wilson, "The Hermit of Heytesbury", www.guardian.co.uk/books/2003/mar/29/featuresreviews.guardianreview28
18 "I was one with Wilfred Owen, though on a lower plane of poetic expression", ibid.
19 Biographical details from Rupert Hart-Davis, *Oxford Dictionary of National Biography* (*DNB*), www.oxforddnb.com/view/article/35953
20 Ibid.
21 Ibid.
22 www.guardian.co.uk/world/2008/nov/10/first-world-war-siegfried-sassoon
23 Siegfried Sassoon, *Memoirs of an Infantry Officer* (Faber, 1930)
24 Hart-Davis, *DNB*
25 Letter to Susan Owen, in Hibberd, *Wilfred Owen*, p. 101
26 Sassoon's comments on the origins of his poetry are included in Rupert Hart-Davis (ed.), *Siegfried Sassoon: The War Poems* (Faber, 1983)
27 Ibid., p. 57
28 Biographical details from Ian Parsons (ed.), *The Collected Works of Isaac Rosenberg* (Chatto & Windus, 1979)
29 Ibid., p. xxii
30 Ibid., p. xxiv
31 Ibid., p. 259
32 Ibid., p. ix
33 Ibid., p. xvii
34 Ibid., p. xvii
35 Ibid., p. ix
36 Ibid., p. 219
37 Figures from BBC, www.bbc.co.uk/history/worldwars/wwone/battle_somme.shtml

38 Parsons, *Isaac Rosenberg*, p. ix
39 Ibid., p. 248
40 Ibid., p. 27
41 Ibid., p. 146
42 Ibid., p. 149
43 Ibid., p. 151
44 ibid., p. 170
45 Ibid., pp. 169–170
46 www.rupertbrookeonskyros.com/Intro.htm
47 The First World War Poetry Digital Archive, www.oucs.ox.ac.uk/ww1lit/
   education/tutorials/intro/brooke/vsoldier.html
48 Ibid., www.oucs.ox.ac.uk/ww1lit/collections/graves
49 Biographical details from www.robertgraves.org
50 "*Good-Bye to All That* by Robert Graves", projects.oucs.ox.ac.uk/jtap/rose/
   goodbye.html
51 www.robertgraves.org/trust/index.php?id=2
52 en.wikipedia.org/wiki/Robert_Graves#cite_note-8
53 Michael Pharand, "Avoiding the Psychoanalytic Confession-Box:
   Robert Graves and W.H.R. Rivers", *Gravesiana*, www.robertgraves.org/
   issues/17/8133_article_387.pdf
54 Robert Graves, *Poems About War* (Cassell, 1988), p. 10
55 Biographical details from Vera Brittain, *Because You Died: Poetry and Prose
   of World War I and After* (ed. Mark Bostridge, Virago, 2008)
56 Ibid., p. 103
57 Ibid., p. 124
58 Ibid., p. 219
59 www.spartacus.schoolnet.co.uk/Jbrittain.htm
60 Biographical details from Hilda D. Spear (ed.), *The Poems and Selected
   Letters of Charles Hamilton Sorley* (Blackness Press, 1978)
61 Letter to the Master of Marlborough, 20 February 1914, in Spear, *Charles
   Hamilton Sorley*, p. 87
62 Letter to A.J. Hopkinson, October 1914, in Spear, *Charles Hamilton Sorley*,
   p. 94
63 Ibid.
64 www.spartacus.schoolnet.co.uk/FWWsorley.htm
65 Spear, *Charles Hamilton Sorley*, p. 9
66 Ibid., p. 26
67 William Archer, introduction to "Poems by Alan Seeger", www.gutenberg.
   org/cache/epub/617/pg617.html
68 Ibid.
69 From "The Aisne"
70 Cross, *Lost Voices*, p. 34
71 Graves, *Poems about War*, p. 10
72 answers.google.com/answers/threadview/id/779825.html
73 From "The Aisne"
74 Cross, *Lost Voices*, p. 3
Biographical details for "Other voices" (pp. 52–55) from *Chambers Biographical
Dictionary*, *The Penguin Book of First World War Poetry* (ed. Jon Silkin, Penguin,
1979), and Cross, *Lost Voices*

INDEX